Robin Tower was forty years old and recently divorced due to severe alcohol abuse. His drinking only escalated after the divorce. He had two adult children who visited regularly. Robin got them to rring well in advance of their visits so that he knew to be sober.

Early one evening, Robin ran out of alcohol and didn't get paid until the next day. He went to bed at 6pm and tossed and turned as he craved alcohol. Eventually he fell asleep.

At exactly 3am, Robin woke up and sat bolt upright. There at the foot of his bed was a glowing, translucent image of a pirate from the 1800s. "Who are you?" Robin exclaimed. The image replied, "I'm a ghost. I am a drowned sailor from 1865. I have been sent to guide you." The ghost had a gentle, soft and polite voice. "Who sent you?" asked Robin. The ghost replied, "Fate."

When he awoke the next morning, Robin had forgotten all about the ghost until he looked at the foot of his bed and there it was. "You! You are real!" The ghost smirked and said, "Yes, Sir. I'm very real." Robin asked, "What are you doing here?" The ghost replied, "Fate sent me here to guide you. I can't tell you what to do but I can advise you. Right now, I'd advise you to have a shower and a shave." Robin was impulsive. Most alcoholics are. He jumped in the shower and had a shave straight away.

Robins main priority was to have a drink. He got into his car and drove to the bottleshop. The ghost sat silently. Robin was jumpy until he had the booze in his car. The ghost floated in the passenger seat, marvelling at this mode of transport. "What's your name ghost?" asked Robin. The ghost replied "Horatio Herald, Sir." Robin then asked, "How come you're a ghost?" Horatio replied, "I was drowned at the mouth of the Bass Strait when we were blown out of the water by pirates in 1865." Robin asked what he had done in the meantime. "I've been in limbo since 1865 until Fate called on me. Everything I see around me is overwhelming."

When Robin sat down and had a drink, Horatio floated around the living room. They had silent, mental conversations. Not a sound was uttered.

After a few drinks, Horatio said to Robin, "I can only advise you, Sir. I can advise you what to do but I can't advise you what NOT to do. You know that you only have one problem in your life.....and it's all-consuming. It is killing you." Robin hung his head and softly said, "Yes....but I don't want to stop. I love being drunk." Horatio replied, "Until you WANT to stop, there"s not much that I can do except keep you in as good a shape as possible."

Robin had taken twelve months off from the legal firm that he worked for with the sole intent of drinking. He had four months before he was due back at work. Eight months to quit the booze and get himself into shape.

Over the next two weeks, Robin showed an enthralled Horatio the wonders of modern technology. He told him about electricity and what it did, the telephone, the television and the wondrous capabilities of the internet which Horatio was captivated by. He also had trouble coming to terms with the fact that the people on the television weren't actually in the room. He just couldn't grasp it.

Horatios' favourite thing, however, was going for a drive to the bottleshop in Robins car. Robin cottoned onto this and decided he would take Horatio for drives. Sometimes out into the country. Horatio marvelled at the scenery. "I've never seen such beauty, Sir. I was raised in the middle of London where it was all houses and buildings. Here you have green fields and there are trees everywhere."

Being an alcoholic, Robin was drunk during all of these journeys. One day, up ahead, he saw two stationary police cars with their lights flashing. "Oh, no," moaned Robin. "What is it, Sir?" asked Horatio. "It's the police. I'm done for." Robin quickly explained what was about to happen.

A police officer signalled for Robin to pull over. He then asked Robin if he had been drinking. "Yes," mumbled Robin who then blew into the breathylizer. He was well over the limit. "Step out of the car please Sir," said the officer. Robin was put in the back of the police car, Horatio followed. They went to the police station where Robin was processed. He was to appear in court the following week. In the meantime he was to pick up his car keys in six hours and make his own way back to his car, which he did....some five miles away.

When they arrived home Robin explained to Horatio what appearing in court meant. Being a lawyer, Robin would represent himself.

When the day of his court appearance arrived, Robin was a bundle of nerves and had quite a few drinks to steady himself. Obviously he pleaded guilty but added that he was under a great deal of stress due to his divorce. The judge took this into consideration and the fact that his blood alcohol reading was mid-range and that this was his first offence (which is a miracle) fined Robin $400 and suspended his license for six months.

On the way back to the car park, Robin and Horatio were mentally talking to each other. "That was lenient," said Robin. As Robin stepped into the car Horatio said, "Sir. The judge banned you from driving." Robin casually replied, "Who cares? As long as I'm careful I'll be alright."

Robin had a point. The only place that he drove to was the bottleshop car park which was only four streets away. These streets were narrow and windding so there was nowhere for the police to set up any checkpoints. It was also a low crime area. Robin had never seen a police car in his travels. The only diversion that he would make was every Thursday when he would ncross the street from the bottleshop car park to the supermarket and do his shopping.

For the first few unlicensed trips to the bottleshop, unlike Robin, Horatio was erather nervous as he looked around for police cars or police on the beat. He soon relaxed.

A few weeks later, one afternoon, Robin fell asleep in his chair clutching a bottle of whiskey. This is something that he had never done before. He awoke with a start to find that he had been incontinent of urine. "That's it!" he exclaimed. "I'm not going to drink again. With that he grabbed his bottle of whiskey and the unopened one on the then poured them both down the sink. "Good for you, Sir!" exclaimed an excited Horatio. "Good for you."

For the next day and a half, Horatio watched as Robin went through the sweats and the shakes that alcoholics do when coming off the drink. Horatio would offer words of support and comfort.

On the third day, Robin started hallucinating and he knew that he was hallucinating. He was having conversations with imaginary people inside the walls of his living room. Then he started talking to a lightbulb. Horatio became extremely distressed by Robins strange behaviour. "Sir," he said. "Yes?" replied Robin. Horatio said, "Don't you think that you should use your telephone and speak to somebody who can help you. You're behaviour is very strange and disturbing." Robin replied, "Yes Horatio. You're right."

Robin went to the phone and said, "Ambulance. Acute alcohol withdrawal," then gave his address. In less than ten minutes an ambulance was on Robins' doorstep. Horatio was initially overwhelmed by the flashing lights and sirens. He was then overwhelmed by the series of questions that one ambulance officer asked Robin. A cuff was put around Robins arm. Robin mentally told Horatio that they were taking his blood pressure. They then inserted a needle into a vein in his arm. Robin mentally told Horatio that this was standard in case they need to give him any drugs quickly. "It's the quickest route," Robin told Horatio.

Robin remained lucid and co-operative in the ambulance on the way to hospital. Horatio was beside himself with concern.

Once at the hospital, Robin was transferred to a bed and wheeled into Accident and Emergency. No sooner was he placed in a cubicle than he began to convulse violently. A medical team surrounded him within seconds. A horrified and scared Horatio put his hands on his cheeks and yelled, "Please help him!" to nobody. A Nurse gave Robin a large dose of intravenous Valium via the needle inserted by the ambulance officer. Horatio remained horrified and afraid. He thought that his friend was going to die.

Within several minutes, Robin was no longer convulsing. He was laying on the bed, very pale and was groggy but coherent when the Nurses asked him a series of questions. A Doctor came in and took a blood sample. He handed it to a Nurse and told her that he wanted the results immediately then left. Horatio remained hovering at the base of Robins' bed.

Fifteen minutes later the Doctor arrived back at Robins' bed holding some pieces of paper. He told Robin that he was lucky in that Robin had minimal liver damage and that it would repair itself provided that he avoid alcohol. He then sat a piece of paper and a business card at the foot of the bed. "You're free to go," he said. "Free to go?" said a shocked Horatio. Robin explained that alcoholics were low on the list of priorities in hospital. "But you're really sick, Sir." Robin shrugged his shoulders, got out of bed, grabbed the pieces of paper left there by the Doctor and headed for the exit. Horatio remained bewildered.

Once at reception, Robin asked if they could call him a taxi. Horatio had never heard this word before. Whilst waiting for the taxi to arrive, Robin explained to Horatio what taxis' did. "What a wonderful idea, Sir," said an enthusiastic Horatio.

When they arrived home, Robin put the pieces of paper on the table without reading them. He collapsed into bed fully clothed. He was exhausted, had suffered a seizure and full of Valium. He slept for twelve hours.

Robin woke up at 11am dazed. He wondered why he had all of his clothes on. He had no recollection of the previous day. He said to Horatio, "What happened yesterday? Please don't tell me I had a drink." Horatio replied, "No you didn't drink, Sir. You went to hospital after hallucinating then you had a seizure." Robin exclaimed, "A seizure?" Horatio then said, "There are a couple of pieces of paper on the table that I think you should read."

Robin groggily made his way through and picked up one of the pieces of paper. It was a prescription for a drug called Campral. Still feeling vague he went to his computer and looked the drug up. It was a drug designed to take away any cravings for alcohol. The only side effects were nausea and dizziness. It said that these side effects were transient. "I can't be bothered going into town today," he told Horatio who disagreed. "Why not strike while the iron's hot, Sir. Let's do it and that'll it be done."

Robin wnt and had a shower, shave and changed his clothes. He and Horatio walked to the nearest tram stop, one which Robin knew all too well. They caught the next tram into the city. Horatio floated up and down the tram, marvelling at the streetscape and all of the people going about their business.

When they got off the tram, Robin had a dilemma. Where to find a pharmacist. He'd never had to use one before. After walking three city blocks he eventually found one. He handed his prescription to the pharmacist who prepared it. On handing Robin the two rather large boxes, he leaned forward and quietly said, "The key to Campral is that you really must want to stop drinking." Robin replied, "Believe me, I do. I've already been to Hell. I don't want to go back." He then asked the pharmacist how long the side effects lasted. "Only two to three days and they're very mild. From what I know it is generally well tolerated."

On arriving home, Robin discovered that there were a hundred tablets in each box and he was to take one a day. He took his first tablet. "Good for you, Sir," said Horatio. Another step forward. Now what about that other piece of paper, Sir?"

Robin picked up the card and it read, 'Cliff Robson. Alcohol Counsellor.' Robin moaned, "Oh, no. What next?" Horatio said, "You want to do everything in your power to stay sober, Sir." Robin reluctantly nodded his head and said, "I know." He slowly made his way to the phone and dialled the number. Cliffs' receptionist booked Robin in for his first appointment the following Friday.

Robin caught the early tram the following Friday in order for him to locate Cliffs' office. As it turned out, the tram stopped right outside Cliffs' office. Robin had two hours to kill. He went and bought a newspaper. As he was reading it he glanced over as he turned a page of the newspaper and spotted a pub. He started shaking and sweating. Horatio noticed this and suggested, "Why don't we go and sit around the corner, Sir?" Robin mentally replied, "Good idea. This is too much."

Ten minutes before his appointment, Robin got upp from his bench and made his way to Cliffs' office. He introduced himself to the secretary who invited him to take a seat, advising him that Cliff wouldn't be long.

Sure enough, two minutes later, a large bald gentleman approached Robin. "You must be Robin," he said. Robin stood up, shook his hand and said, "I am." Cliff said, "Follow me." Robin followed Cliff down a corridor and ushered him into his office where he offered Robin to take a seat. Cliff was very laid back in his manner but it was obvious that he knew his stuff and more importantly, obvious to Robin that he was genuine.

Cliff did the majority of talking for the hour long session, asking Robin how long he had been drinking for, how much and how had alcohol impacted Robins' life. He was also sizing Robin up. Finding out if he was genuine. Robin actually thought when he was being questioned, 'I may as well tell the truth. I'm here for help after all.'

At the close of the session Cliff said, "You still want to drink, don't you?" Robin said, "Yes I do." Cliff handed him a business card which read, 'Leroy. Alcoholics Anonymous.' Robin looked at Cliff. They're a good bunch of people. They've all been through what you've been through. Give James a ring and find out where and when their meetings are held. In the meantime, our programme will run at the same time every Friday for three months. You've made another big step forward Robin," and shook his hand.

On arriving home, Robin slumped down in his chair and sighed. Horatio knew something wasn't right with Robin. "What's wrong, Sir?" he asked. Robin replied, "Cliff's a good an knowledgeable man." He paused before continuing, "But I don't know if I'm going to get any further benefit from seeing him every week for three months." Horatio fired back, "You don't know how much more knowledge he has to impart....and if nothing else it will give you something to do." Robin agreed. "I guess so."

For the next two days Horatio watched Robin alternately paced, wriggled in his seat, did online crosswords and would lay down frequently. They had both forgotten the Alcoholics Anonymous card until Robin accidentally knocked it off the kitchen bench. He instantly picked it up and rang the number. He gave his first name and asked when and where their meetings were. The meetings were held every Thursday night at 7.30 at the church not more than four hundred metres away.

The next week was a long and angsty one but with the aid of Campral, Horatio and willpower, Robin didn't drink.

When the day of the Alcoholics Anonymous arrived Robin was the edgiest that Horatio had seen him. He went to his cupboard several times. 'Should I dress up? Should I dress down? How should I dress?' he thought. Horatio suggested that Robin should dress smart casual. "Smart casual it is," agreed Robin.

When they arrived at the church, both doors were open. The large hall was dimly lit and chairs were set out in a semi-circle. When Robin walked in, nobody batted an eyelid. He stood there feeling quite awkward. After a few moments a large black man said, "Let's get this show on the road." At that, people took a seat. Robin awkwardly took a seat. A lady sitting next to him smiled at him. Robin nervously smiled back.

When everybody was settled the large black man began to speak. "My name's Leroy and I'm an alcoholic. I've been sober for twenty years thanks to this building and the people in it." He received a round of applause. The person in the next seat as Leroy had. "I'm (such and such) and I'm an alcoholic." They would then go on to tell their story. Robin heard some real shockers. Some made him look tame.

After everybody had spoken, they made their way to the coffee machine. Leroy made his way over to Robin and said, "So you're Robin. Welcome, man. Do you have any questions?" Robin, half under his breath, said, "I can smell alcohol, Leroy." Leroy replied, "We're all human. Humans make mistakes and sometimes alcoholics make mistakes. We're here to pick them up and support them. Not to judge them." Robin smiled and said, "I like that, Leroy." Leroy laughed and patted Robin on the shoulder.

Over the next forty five minutes, every single member at the meeting made a point of introducing themselves to Robin and having a chat about this and that. Robin ended up thoroughly enjoying himself. On the walk home and for about two hours after arriving home, Robin raved about how much he enjoyed himself.

The following morning Robin had his meeting with Cliff. The first question Cliff asked Robin was if he had been in touch with Alcoholics Anonymous. "I did," said Robin. A smile came to Cliffs face. He sat back in his chair, put his hands behind his head, leaned back and asked, "How did you go?" This was like holding a red rag to a bull. Robin raved on about it for half an hour. He concluded by saying, "That Leroy is some bloke." Clive said, "He is." A surprised Robin said, "You know him?" Cliff said, "I've known him for twenty years. I remember his first night there." Cliff saw Robin looking puzzled, "I used to attend Alcoholics Anonymous. I'm an alcoholic but had to leave when I landed this job as some members there are clients of mine here. Conflict of interest and all that." Robin was gobsmacked by both the story and by Cliffs' honesty.

"Well Robin. You're off to a flying start....but you've still got a long way to go. You know that, don't you?" Robin said, "Oh, yes." Clive went on to add that the full effect of the Campral will kick in in a week. "It'll be a long week but you have Alcoholics Anonymous and me to look forward to at the end of it." He added, "Get through this week and you've taken a huge leap forward."

It was indeed a long and unpleasant week for Robin. He was edgy, shaking, pacing and intermittently laying down. He was dying for a drink. Horatio was offering words of encouragement and comfort with eventual effect. On Thursday afternoon Robin began to feel different. Horatio noticed that Robin was more settled. He wasn't shaking, sweating, pacing or laying down. He was quite content doing online crosswords. He said, "Do you know what Horatio?" Horatio replied, "What's that, Sir?" Robin replied, "I don't feel like a drink. The Campral must be working." Horatio was ecstatic and said, "Don't just thank the Campral, Sir. YOUR willpower has a big say in it."

That night at the Alcoholics Anonymous meeting, Robin told everybody how he felt. He received a huge round of applause. At the end of the meeting Leroy told him that even though he had made a great step forward he still had a long way to go. "One day at a time, Robin," said Leroy. "One day at a time....but great news, my man."

The following day at his appointment with Cliff he told him his good news. Cliff was pleased for Robin, telling him he had taken another step forward but not to look too far ahead. "One day at a time, Robin. One day at a time." Robin smirked as he recalled Leroy say the exact same thing.

At a few Alcoholics Anonymous meetings later, an elderly lady eyeballed Robin, came up to him and re-introduced herself as Anne. She took Robin by the arm and led him away from the group, looked around suspiciously and then whispered, "Do you believe in ghosts?" Robin replied, "Yes. Yes I do." Anne said, "I thought so. I'm psychic you see and I can sense a spirit close to you. I've sensed it at every meeting."

Robin said to Anne, "Look, I only live four hundred metres from here. Would you like to come up and we could discuss the matter." Anne replied, "Oh, I wouldn't want to out you out." Robin replied, "You wouldn't be putting me out at all." Anne agreed.

 They spoke mainly about alcohol but half way there Anne stopped. "What is it?" asked Robin. Ann said, "I sense a spirit very close to me." Robin smirked. Horatio was floating right next to Anne. Robin laughed and said, "I'll explain everything when we get back to my place." Anne replied, "Oh, I'm intrigued. I can't wait."

When they arrived at Robins, Ann took a seat. Robin made the pair a coffee and took a seat himself. Robin asked Ann how long she had been psychic. Ann replied, "As long as I can remember. I've seen countless ghosts and spirits." Robin asked if she was ever afraid of these ghosts. Ann laughed, "Oh goodness no. Ghosts won't hurt you." Anne then turned the tables on Robin and asked if he had ever seen a ghost. Robin replied, "Oh, yes. I'm looking at one right now." He was looking at the kitchen where Horatio was looking on and listening.

Ann then asked Robin if he would mind asking the ghost if it would make itself visible to her. Robin looked at Horatio and asked him, "Horatio. Would you make yourself visible to Anne. She's familiar with ghosts." Horatio floated over to the living room and said, "I know, Sir. I heard."

Horatio stood at the other end of the coffee table from Anne and made himself visible to her. Anne didn't bat an eyelid and said, "Hello Horatio. It's a pleasure to meet you." Horatio removed his hat and bowed. "It's a pleasure to make your acquaintance too, ma'am."

Anne asked Horatio all sorts of questions. "How old were you when you died?" Horatio replied, "I was thirty years old, ma'am." Anne said, "Please call me Anne." She then asked how he died. Horatio said, "We were attacked by a pirate ship at the heads of the Bass Strait near Tasmania. We were out-gunned. The ship sank and all crew were lost. My parents found out two years later."

Anne went on to ask about his family. "I was the middle child of twelve. It was a poor upbringing. I joined the Navy for a better life when I was fifteen years old."

Horatio asked Anne about herself. "I'm married with one son. He's a mechanic." Horatio asked what a mechanic was. When Anne told him, Horatio was amazed. "He can make motor cars go. That's quite amazing. He must be a genius." Ann laughed and said, "He's a bright boy alright. We don't see him much. He lives in another state. Still on his own." Robin said with a wry smile, "He *is* a bright boy." Ann and Horatio laughed.

Anne then asked Horatio why he came to Robin. Horatio said, "Fate. Robin was having a rough time and needed guidance. I'm here to guide him." Anne said, "How long will you be here for, Horatio?" Horatio answered, "I'll be here for as long as Robin is alive because he will always be an alcoholic." Anne nodded and finished her coffee.

"Oh well," Anne said. "I'd better go. My husband will be wondering where I am," she laughed. "Thank you for your invitation, Robin and it was a real pleasure to meet you Horatio. Maybe we'll meet again." Horatio replied, "Likewise Anne."

Robin offered to walk her back but Anne declined. "I'm sure I can find my way," she said with a laugh.

Two weeks later saw Robins last meeting with Cliff. Instead of going for the usual hour it lasted two hours as they discussed baseball, basketball and how soccer was really taking off, with America just having qualified for the World Cup. Cliff had some parting advice for Robin. He said, "You've done extremely well my man. One of my best clients but in the grand scheme of things you have only been sober for a short time....but you're on the right track. You have the right mindset." On his way out the door, Cliff handed Robin his private mobile number. "Remember, Robin. You're never alone. You use that number any time that you need to. Robin thanked him and said, "I hope I don't need to use it." Cliff said, "Me too....but if you feel the need, don't hesitate."

Robin felt that he had really achieved something....and he had. He received a round of applause at Alcoholics Anonymous when he told them about successfully completing the course with Cliff.

Robin was on a high for ages. Too high. One night, out of the blue, he grabbed the car keys and jumped in the car. Horatio had a feeling what was coming next and didn't like that feeling. "Sir! Sir! What are you doing," he said to Robin. Robin remained silent, eyes focussed on the road. Horatio continued, "You're doing so well, Sir. You've come so far. Please don't ruin it now, Sir." Robin remained silent as he drove to the bottleshop and bought two bottles of whiskey.

When they arrived home, Robin opened the first bottle and threw the lid away. He drank it at breakneck speed as a smile spread across his face and his cheeks glowed. He was talking jibberish to Horatio who simply agreed with him as he knew there was no point in trying to reason with somebody who is drunk.

This would be the beginning of a three day bender that would come to a sudden halt. On day two he rang Cliff, drunk. Cliff thanked him for calling and referred him to Leroy. He rang Leroy who calmly advised hi, "Nobody can stop but you, man. I can't even come over there and make you stop. You'll stop when you need to stop."

That 'need to stop' came on the third day of Robins' bender when he went to the toilet and vomited massive amounts of blood. It looked like red paint. "I need an ambulance," he gasped to Horatio. Horatio said, "That you do, Sir."

When the ambulance arrived, Robin staggered with the assistance of the ambulance officers into the ambulance. It was obvious from the blood on Robins' face what the problem was. Horatio watched on as an officer handed Robin a vomit bag while the other inserted an intravenous needle into his arm. They then injected him with a drug called Maxolon which is an anti-emetic. It had little effect as Robin vomited again.

On arriving in Casualty he was placed on a bed and wheeled into a booth. Robin was as white as a sheet. Horatio looked on, concerned.

The Doctor didn't have to look far to find the problem. At the back of Robins' throat was a massive oesophageal tear caused from violent vomiting. The blood running out of the tear was going straight to Robins' stomach which was making him vomit more. They took blood samples from him.

Immediately they commenced intravenous Omeprazole to help heal the oesophageal tear. When the blood results returned it was discovered, not surprisingly, that Robin was anaemic. Another intravenous needle was inserted into his other arm and he was taken to the ward. Horatio looked on anxiously.

After about thirty minutes a Nurse came into Robin's ward wielding a bag of blood. She introduced herself then proceeded to explain that Robin was going to have a blood transfusion as his blood count was (unsurprisingly) low. He was to have three bags and his blood count would be repeated in the morning.

While all three blood bags were running, a Nurse would come in and check his pulse, temperature and blood pressure every fifteen minutes. Horatio looked on, offering words of encouragement. "I know it's hard," said Horatio, "But you've made a mistake. You're human. Just like Leroy said. Robin couldn't say much to Horatio or the Nurses would think that he was mad. He discretely relayed this to Horatio who said, "I understand, Sir."

After the three bags of blood had ran through, Robin was given an intravenous sedative. It had no effect and he spent a restless, shaky and sweaty night. This was pure anxiety.

The following morning a Doctor came in and examined Robins throat. Fifteen minutes later a Nurse came in and took the bag of Omeprazole down. An hour later Robin had his blood taken. Two hours later a Nurse came into Robins' ward wielding a piece of paper. She advised Robin that his blood count was fine and handed him the piece of paper. "You've been discharged," she said. "Take this prescription to the hospital pharmacy. It's Omeprazole in tablet form. Be sure to take the whole course."

Robin got dressed, found the hospital pharmacy and picked up his prescription. He then went outside and found the bus terminal and looked at the timetable. Looking at it he discovered that he had an hour to wait.

There was nobody at the bus stop so Robin and Horatio could speak feely, although Robin wasn't in a talking mood. Horatio continued to encourage him. "You made a mistake, Sir. Remember Leroy daid that humans make mistakes." Robin replied, "Don't remind me. I've got an Alcoholics Anonymous meeting tonight. I don't want to go. What will I tell them?" Horatio replied, "Tell them the truth. They're there to support you." Robin said, "But it'll be embarrassing." Horatio fired back, "They're there to support you, not criticise you." Robin fell silent again.

When they arrived home, Robin spent the afternoon pacing, sitting down for a few minutes, getting up and pacing again, continually looking at his watch, drinking water, looking at his watch, sweating and shaking. He was a nervous wreck. This wasn't alcohol withdrawal. Robin hadn't drank enough over a long enough period to display classic alcohol withdrawal symptoms.

When the time came, Robin made his way to the Alcoholics Anonymous meeting. Horatio continued to encourage him. Robin was silent. When he entered the building, it was obvious to all that something was wrong with Robin. People started speaking but Robin was a thousand miles away as he fidgeted and shuffled in his seat.

When it came his turn to speak, you could feel the anticipation in the room. A sense of 'calm' washed over Robin. He gave a blow by blow account of recent events. There was an audible gasp around the room When he finished he received a round of applause Leroy said, "You're here, man. You're here."

When the speeches were over and the coffees were being had, every single person made a point of shaking Robins hand or patting him on the back. They asked if he was alright physically and that it wasn't a crime to have a slip. The important thing was that he made it to Alcoholics Anonymous. Anne pulled him aside and whispered, "I bet Horatio was a great help." Robin replied, "He was indeed Anne."

With his drivers license returned to him, Robin now had a looming fear. He was becoming uneasy and Horatio knew it. Eventually Horatio asked, "What's on your mind? Is it alcohol?" Robin said, "No. I'm due back at work soonand I'm worried about how I'll be received." Horatio reassured him. "You'll be fine, Sir. You're sharper than ever and lokk a whole lot better than when you took leave. This did indeed reassure Robin and gave him confidence. "Thank you, Horatio," he said. My pleasure," said Horatio. That's what I'm here for." Horatio was keen to see Robin at work.

Robin had all his suits, shirts and ties ready and shoes shone a week in advance.

On his way to work, Robins heart was pounding. Horatio knew it and reassured him. When Robin arrived at work, his old parking spot was there waiting for him. His pulse dropped. As soon as he entered the building of his law firm he felt the same feeling of 'calm' come over him like it did at Alcoholics Anonymous when he told the members about his slip and subsequent hospitalisation.

When he walked into the offices he was warmly welcomed by the staff and complimented on how well he looked. "How's the divorce going?" asked one staff member. There was a deafening silence. Robin promptly replied, "Going fine. We didn't go through the courts. Everything's amicable."

There was one staff member that Robin didn't recognise. She hung back from his known work colleagues. Robin went over to her. She was buxom and curvaceous and looked to be a couple of years younger than Robin. Robin reached out his hand and they shook hands, "Hi. I'm Robin." He noticed that she hadn't let go of her grip on his hand. "Hi. I'm Andrea," she said before adding, "It's a pleasure to meet you. I've heard a lot about you," then she winked at him. Robin gave her a warm smile.

Robins' boss gave him a light case-load to start with. He didn't want to throw him in the deep end but Robin was razor sharp and things got the better of him half way through his second week back. He approached his boss and asked for more cases. "Are you sure you're up to it, Robin?" he said. Robin reassured him that he was up to the task. "I haven't felt so sharp in years, Sir." His boss replied, "Very well Robin."

With a full case-load Robin was now in full flight. Horatio was amazed at Robins' expertise and particularly his manner in court.

A month after Robin started back at work his legal firm held a formal party at a local venue. Robin was rather looking forward to it.

On arrival, in the foyer, waitresses were carryin trays with flutes of champagne and glasses of what appeared to be orange juice. Robin grabbed an orange juice only to discover that it had gin in it. He hesitated for a second then downed it and had another. By the time people went to the dining area, Robin was tipsy. Every time a waitress went past, Robin would grab two gins. When he began talking loudly, Horatio knew that something wasn't right.

As the night progressed Horatio knew that Robin was drunk as he was slurring his words. Robin noticed Andrea, who was also drunk, batting her eyelids at him. Robin started winking at her. By the end of the night, Robin and Andrea were the only two on the dance floor. They were doing a waltz....to rap music. Robin whispered in Andreas' ear if she would like to come to his place for a coffee. She agreed.

After a giggling tram journey they arrived at Robins. They laughed and joked until 3am. Out of the blue Robin said, "I have a confession to make, Andrea." Andrea leaned forward and said, "Do tell." Robin said, "I'm an alcoholic and I've just made a mistake." Andrea looked non-plussed and said, "Same here." Robin was taken aback and didn't know what to say. Andrea ended up staying the night.

The following morning when they woke up, Robin and Andrea had shocking hangovers. They were both sweating, shaking and holding their heads. Robin made them both a coffee. As they were having their coffee, Robin asked Andrea how long she had been an alcoholic. Andrea had to think. "I'm not sure," she said. "Probably about five years." Robin then asked what support mechanism she used. Andrea said, "I don't." Robin couldn't believe it. "You need some support, Andrea," who replied, "Where from?" Robin suggested Alcoholics Anonymous. "You could come to meetings with me if you like. It's been really helpful for me." Andrea thought about it for a while then said, "Okay. I'll give it a try." Robin told her where and when the meetings were held.

Robin then drove Andrea home. She lived only a few kilometres away. When they arrived at Andreas' house Robin offered to pick her up and take her to meetings. "That's very kind of you. Thank you," said Andrea. Robin replied, "It will be my pleasure....In the meantime, I guess I'll see you at work on Monday." Andrea said, "I guess you will." Robin leaned over to give Andrea a peck on the cheek. It ended up being a rather long embrace.

Robin arrived home full of beans. "Not a word, Horatio. Not a word." Horatio replied, "I was only going to congratulate you, Sir. You could do with a bit of romance in your life," then winked at Robin who smiled broadly back. "Yes. You're quite right Horatio. Andrea has put a real spring in my step."

The following Monday at work, Robin didn't encounter Andrea until about 10am. Andrea immediately blushed noticeably. Robin said, "Good morning Andrea," then added with a cheeky grin, "How was your weekend?" Andrea replied, "Hi Robin. My weekend was fabulous thank you." Robin invited to have lunch with him. "I'd love to," she said.

When lunch-time came they went to a nearby cafe'. There was no awkwardness and conversation and laughter flowed freely. Then Andrea leaned forward and whispered what Robin had been waiting for. "What happens at these Alcoholics Anonymous meetings?"

Robin explained that members sat around in a circle and told their story. "I don't think I could do that." Robin then explained that every member had been where they had been. "They're not there to judge or persecute. They're there to support."

When Thursday night came, Robin picked Andrea up as arranged. She leaned over and kissed him. Robin smiled. On the way to the meeting it was obvious that Andrea was a bundle of nerves. "Relax," said Robin. "I was the same but by the end of the very first meeting I'd made a dozen new friends. Friends who were there to support me. Friends who really did know what it was like." This put Andreas' mind at ease slightly but shhe was still (understandably) on edge.

They entered the building and took a seat. Leroy, as usual, started the ball rolling. When it came to Robins' turn he confessed to his partly accidental slip on Friday. "I didn't know there was gin in the orange juice....but when I did I couldn't get enough. I ended up waltzing on the dance floor to rap music." Anne said, "The exact same thing happened to me at an art exhibition. I had to be helped out. It was most embarrassing." This put Andreas' mind at rest.

It was Andreas' turn next.

"My name is Andrea and I'm an alcoholic. I think I've been an alcoholic for about five years. It was causing problems at work and causing problems at home with my parents. I was also in financial trouble because of alcohol. One day I looked at myself and told myself I was an alcoholic and that only I could sort it. I was wrong. I don't know how many failed attempts I've had at getting sober....Oh! I was the person waltzing to rap music with Robin." Andrea blushed again as she received a round of applause.

After the meeting and on the way to Andreas' house, Robin asked, "Will you be back?" Andrea said, "Sure." Robin invited Andrea to his place for a coffee. She accepted. They spoke mainly about work and office politics. These Thursday night coffees became a ritual. Horatio was thrilled, telling Robin what a wonderful girl Andrea was and how they made a great couple. "I wouldn't say we're a couple Horatio," before adding, "Yet." The pair smirked.

One day Robin had a new client. A Mr. Jones. He told his receptionist to send him through. There was a knock on the door. "Come in." In walked none other than Leroy carrying a manilla folder. "Hi Leroy. How can I help you?" Leroy was obviously in pain.

He explained to Robin that two nights ago, he was walking past a night club when two policemen pushed him to the ground and began kicking him. Leroy managed to stand up and swing two punches. One at each officer. The next thing he knew was that a squad car pulled up, four policemen jumped out and Leroy was arrested for Grievous Bodily Harm. He was drug tested, breathalyzed and strip searched.

Leroy's a bright boy. He immediately went back to the night club and obtained four witness statements and the CCTV footage of the incident. He then called an ambulance, got taken to hospital and had his bruised torso photographed and a Doctors report written.

All of these were in the manilla folder that Robin was beginning to browse through, grinning. "Well, Leroy," he said, "You've just made my job so easy. It's the police who have a case to answer here not you. A blind man could see that. Leroy breathed a sigh of relief. "You can relax, Leroy. This is a cakewalk. When do we roll? Leroy said, "Three weeks," and handed Robin the court document. "Okay," said Robin. "9.30. You meet me at the courthouse at 9.15 for a brief pep talk. You don't have to say a thing once we're in there."

When Robin and Andrea attended the next Alcoholic
Anonymous meeting, Leroy made a bee-line for
Robin. He greeted him warmly and winked, "Hey
Robin. My man. How's it going?" Robin leaned up to
Leroy and said, "Follow me home. It's only four
hundred metres away." Andrea noticed Leroy wink
and instantly suspected that something was going on
between Leroy and Robin.

At the end of the meeting Robin and Andrea were
chatting. Robin asked Andrea if she would mind
having a coffee with him and Leroy at Robins' house.
"Sure," said Andrea. Then Leroy came over to the
pair and was about to start chatting. "Not here," said
Robin. "It's a legal matter that I want to discuss with
you and Andrea. Andrea is a lawyer at my legal firm.'
Leroy nodded his head and the three left.

When they arrived at Robins' house, Robin made
them all a coffee. Robin then explained Leroys
situation and showed her Leroys' evidence. "They
should be charged," said Andrea. "Exactly," said
Robin. Robin said that he felt the police would drop
the charges as soon as the Prosecutor was handed
Leroys' evidence. Robin asked Leroy if he would be
prepared to press charges against the police officers.
Leroy was reluctant at first then Andrea said, "It's a
racial crime, Leroy." Leroy agreed.

Leroy then looked at Robin and Andrea and smirked.
Robin asked, "What?" Leroy then said, "Are you
guys.....you know.....are you?" Simultaneously Robin
and Andrea said, "Sort of." All three laughed.

Sure enough, as Robin expected, a letter came in from the Police Departmente

Andrea was lost for words. As her coffee cup she had to put it down. "Don't worry Ma'am. I can't hurt you." Questions began to come out of Andrea. "How old are you? Where are you from? How did you die? What are you doing here?"

It was the answer to the last question that interested Horatio the most. "I'm here to help Robin. I was just over a year ago." Andrea said, "Who sent you?" Horatio replied, "Fate." This made sense to Andrea. "I wish I had a ghost," she said. "You can have me when things get rough Ma'am." said Horatio. Both Robin and Andrea were surprised at the offer.

After returning home from dropping Andrea off Robin asked Horatio about his offer to Andrea. "You're almost out of the woods with alcohol, Sir. It's early days for Andrea. She needs keeping an eye on. YOU should remember that too, Sir." Robin nodded and rubbed his chin. Horatio was right and it was very generous of him.

Robin acknowledged Horatios' generosity and told him. He asked Horatio why he offered to keep an eye on Andrea and how he would go about it. Horatio said that he would alternate his time between Robins' house and Andreas' house.

Robin then asked how he knew that Andrea wasn't out of the woods as far as alcohol was concerned. Horatio replied, "Well she has only just sought help and I know that she still has cravings." Robin asked how he knew this. Horatio replied, "I'm a ghost, remember Sir. I have supernatural powers. Andrea is a very intelligent lady with a bubbly personality. She finds covering up easy."

From then on, Horatio told Robin that he would spend time at Andreas' from 5pm until 9pm each night except for meeting nights. Robin asked why these times. Horatio said, "It's the time when she finishes work and feels like a drink most and 9pm is when the bottleshop opens." He went on to add that he imagined he would be spending less time at Andreas as Andrea would be spending more time at Robins in the future.

The time came for Leroys' court case. It was scheduled for 10.30am. Robin called him from his office the day before and told him to meet him at the courthouse at 10.15am.

Leroy presented at the courthouse right on 10.15. Robin took him into a side room and told him, "This will be a cakewalk. You don't have to say a thing. Just sit there, look glum and let me do all of the talking. Don't look at the defence.

When they were called, Robin and Leroy entered the courtroom. A policeman held the door open for them. Leroy said nothing as directed by Robin. As Robin stood and sorted his papers, Leroy sat and looked at the floor. He did this for the entire proceedings.

The Judge looked and indicated for Robin to commence. "Your Honour, my client Mr. Jones, a *black* man was pushed to the ground by two *white* police officers and viciously kicked in the ribs." Robin passed the hospital photographs of Leroys' badly bruised ribs.

Robin continued. "Mr. Jones somehow got to his feet and to *defend* himself against TWO armed policemen swung one punch only at each officer. That's not all, Your Honour. The POLICE had the audacity to press charges against my client. My client had the presence of mind to collect six witness statements." Robin handed the statements to the Judge who (surprisingly) read them all. "There's more, Your Honour," Robin continued. "My client has DVD footage of the incident." Robin handed the DVD to the Judge who watched it with a look of disgust on his face.

Robin concluded by saying, "Interestingly, Your Honour, the police prosecution dropped their charges TWO DAYS after receiving the evidence that I have just presented to you. I rest my case."

The Police Department pleaded no contest. In handing down his sentence the Judge aired his disgust not only at the two officers involved but at the Police Department for having the audacity to press charges then drop them in the face of the truth. "I take both crimes very seriously," yelled the Judge. He looked at the two officers and said, "Stand up!" He continued, "You are a disgrace to the uniform and in my opinion are not fit to be called policemen. Your employment is terminated. To the Police Department he called for a major management change to be overseen by an independent body. "Heads will roll!' To Mr. Jones, I apologise on behalf of the legal system and award you a $1,200 Victims Of Crime payment to be paid, in cash, within fourteen days."

Outside of the sourthouse Leroy gave Robin a bear hug. Robin thought that he was going to break his ribs. Leroy let Robin go and vigorously shook his hand, saying, "See you Thursday, man." Robin in turn replied, "See you Thursday, Leroy."

At the following Alcoholics meeting Leroy spotted Robin and Andrea walking in and made a bee-line for Robin. "Hi Andrea and how are you this evening?" in a very polite voice. Andrea was a little surprised and said, "I'm fine, thank you Leroy." Leroy then turned to Robin and shook his hand vigorously, "How's my man?" Robin replied, "Fine Leroy. I wonder why you're in such a good mood." Leroy laughed and said, "I wonder why that would be, Robin." They both laughed. Andrea was confused but knew that something was going on between the two.

After the meeting, Robin invited Andrea and Leroy to his house for a coffee. "It's only four hundred meetings away, Leroy." They both accepted Robins' invitation.

They arrived at Robins's house and Robin made them all coffees. They chatted for a while when Robin said, "Leroy. Andrea is a lawyer too. Would you mind if I went through your case with her? I have all of the evidence in my briefcase." Leroy replied, "Sure, man." Robin went and grabbed his suitcase. He then got Leroy to tell Andrea his story. Andrea couldn't believe it.

Robin then opened his briefcase and handed the witness statements to Andrea. She read them with ever-widening eyes. "It gets me better," said Robin who put on the CCTV footage on his television. Andrea was flabbergasted and said To Robin, "That must be the easiest case that you've had, Robin." Robin laughed and said, "It was. Leroy did all the work. They all laughed. Andrea couldn't believe her ears when Robin told her that *the police* actually pressed charges and dropped them a few days after I lodged our evidence. "They what?" exclaimed Andrea.

Andrea turned to Leroy and complimented him on having the courage and initiative to take the actions that he did. "I just did what I thought was right, Andrea. A man has to defend himself."

While Andrea and Leroy were talking, Robin looked at Horatio and began raising his eyebrows and nodding towards Leroy. Horatio smiled and nodded.

When there was a lull in conversation, Robin leaned forward and said to Leroy, "Do you believe in ghosts Leroy?" Leroy leaned back and casually said, "Why sure I do, man. I even think I've seen a couple." Robin said, "Do you want to see another one?" Leroy laughed and said, Get out of here, man." At that Robin said, "Horatio!"

Horatio floated over to the middle of the room, faced Leroy and Andrea and made himself forward. Leroy leaned forward, put his chin in his hands and said "Hot damn! A real ghost." Horatio did his customary greeting, removed his hat, bowed and said, "Horatio Herald. It's a pleasure to meet you Leroy. You are obviously a good man." Leroy leaned forward and asked Horatio, "Can I touch you?" Horatio laughed and said, "You can try Leroy." Leroy got up and went to gently poke Horatio in the chest. His hand went straight through. Leroy sat down.

"Hot damn. A real ghost in front of my very eyes." He turned to Andrea and asked her if she already knew. Andrea nodded. Leroy then spoke to both Robin and Andrea. He leaned forthright an alternated his eye contact between the pair. He began, "I hope you don't mind me asking but......but, erm," Andrea interjected, "Yes we are." Leroy exclaimed, "Yes! I knew it. Youu guys make a great couple." He asked id it interfered with their work. "Andrea said, "Not at all. We're not that serious.....yet," then looked and smiled at Robin who smiled back.

They continued to chat. Leroy said to Horatio, "Come sit next to me, man." Horatio floated over, sat next to Leroy and joined in the conversation. Leroy asked if he came to meetings. "I do," said Horatio. Leroy asked Horatio what he thought of the meetings. Horatio replied, "I think they're a wonderful thing, Leroy. I've seen a huge change in Robin since he's started attending." Leroy said, "So have I."

When it came time to leave, Robin offered to take Andrea and Leroy home. Leroy refused the offer initially saying that he's rather walk. Robin convinced him to take a lift.

It turned out that Leroy lived on the far side of town in a rough area. He got Robin to drop him off outside a large apartment block. "See you next week," said Leroy. Robin and Andrea echoed, "See you next week."

On the way back over to Andreas' her and Robin wondered why Leroy came from all the way across town to the meetings. They came up with a lot of theories but they were all wrong. When Robin dropped Andrea off they embraced for a long time. Robin drove home thinking what Andrea had said at his place. "Yet."

The next day Robin had a dozen red roses delivered to Andrea at work. On the card was written, 'Anonymous.' Andrea blushed amidst her work colleagues but knew that the flowers were from Robin. 'Anonymous' was a give-away. Andrea knew who they were from. Robin carried on as if nothing had happened. "Nice flowers," he casually said.

After the next meeting, Leroy beat Robin to Robin and Andreas' burning question. He said to Robin, "Can I come to your place after the here, I'd like to meet Horatio again. Robin said, "Sure."

They arrived at Robins house and while

Robin was making coffees he said to Horatio, "It's okay to make yourself visible and take a seat." Horatio replied, "Thank you, Sir." He made himself visible, floated onto the couch next to Leroy and said, "Hello," to Andrea and Leroy who greeted him in return. After they had been chatting for a while, Robin came straight out and said, "Leroy, why do you come all the way across town?" Leroy explained, "The Alcoholics Anonymous meetings over that way are anything but. Everybody knows every alcoholic and it's a hot-bed of gossip. I need privacy." Robin, Andrea and Horatio nodded. "It sounds to me," said Horatio, "that you all need privacy. A place where you can be totally honest and make mistakes without fear of reprisals." Leroy said, "That's exactly right Horatio."

Robin offered to take Andrea and Leroy home. Andrea said she'd like to stay a while. Leroy and Horatio smirked. Leroy refused the offer saying that he now had the connecting tram timetable.

Robin, Andrea and Horatio sat down again after Leroy left. With a mock annoyed face she said to Robin, "Those flowers, Robin." Robin played dumb and said, "Yes?" Andrea said, "They were sent from 'Anonymous.' You're 'Anonymous.' You didn't send them did you?" Robin smirked and said, "Certainly not." They both knew that he was lying.

Robin then invited Andrea to a walk in the park the following Saturday. "I'm not much one for going out to dinner I'm afraid," said Robin. "Neither am I," said Andrea. "I'm not into the stuffy formal scene."

There was a lake with a duck enclosure at one end just a short drive from Robins.' Robin would pick up Andrea at 2pm and drive to the park. Robin had the presence of mind to bring a bag of bread. As they walked around the lake, Robin and Andreas' hands brushed together. They ended up holding hands. They looked at each other and smiled.

When they arrived at the duck enclosure, Robin held the bread bag open so that he and Andrea could feed the ducks. "It must be great being a duck," said Robin. "Why's that?" asked Andrea. Robin replied, "You can walk, float effortlessly, fly if you want and get fed by idiots like us." Andrea laughed. "You're right. I've never thought about ducks like that. You've got too much time on your hands," and kept laughing. Robin said, "No. Seriously. It's all part of nature. Some animals can walk and fly. Some can swim....but not many   fly, float, walk and get fed. If I come back I want to come back as a duck." They spent three hours at the park.

On the walk back to the car, Robin asked Andrea, "How about grabbing a pizza later?" Andrea enthusiastically replied, "Sure." Robin said, "I'll just have to duck into the supermarket on the way home. I'll only be a minute." Andrea replied, "That's okay."

Robin found a place in the busy car park, quite a walk from the supermarket and darted towards it. Andrea rolled down her window and yelled to him, "There's no rush! We've got all night!" Robin quickly turned and grinned.

The supermarket was packed. Robin grabbed chips, nachos, dip, biscuits and nuts for the pair to nibble on that night. Being a bachelor he didn't have things like that at home. He got to the checkouts and they were loaded with people so he went to the self-serve. He unpacked his bag but accidentally left two containers of dip in his bag meaning he wouldn't have paid for them.

Robin didn't discover this until he unpacked the bag when he got home and checked the receipt. He panicked. "Don't worry about it, Robin. It was an honest mistake. Heaps of people would have done it." Robin replied, "They've got security cameras. They'll pick me up." Andrea replied, "They never check those things. Relax."

The pair spent the evening drinking coffee and nibbles when Andrea said, "Let's get that pizza." Robin got on the phone and ordered a pizza and a large bottle of Coca Cola. When the pizza arrived they devoured it in no time. They spent the rest of their time chatting and mainly laughing. Andrea ended up spending the night.

Robin woke up in the night to go to the toilet, he sneaked to Andreas' side of the bed and tried one o her rings on and found that they fitted his pinkie Robin had bigger plans.

The following moning Robin suggested to Andrea that they make Saturdays just like the previous day Andrea said, "Sure. Just like a date." Robin said "Yeah. Just like a date." Andrea said, You're on." The pair smiled at each other.

After six months of these 'dates' the pair got to know each other very well. They had no secrets and were always up-front with each other. Robin decided to take the final step. One Saturday night at his place he said to Andrea, "Oh! I've got something for you," and disappeared into his bedroom leaving Andrea wondering what it could possibly be.

Robin returned and placed a shoebox on the table. "Shoes?" said Andrea. "Just open it," said Robin gently. When Andrea opened the shoebox, there was a small jewellery box in it. Andreas' eyes widened. She opened the small box and there appeared a beautiful diamond ring. Andreas' jaw dropped. Robin then said, "Andrea, will you marry me?" Andrea burst into tears and then ran over to Robins' chair and embraced him. "Of course I will," she sobbed.

The pair officially announced their impending marriage when they went to work the following Monday. There were hugs, hand shakes and pats on the back all round.

Robin spent the day ringing here there and everywhere to organise an informal and outdoor wedding. By 5pm, everything was organised. Andrea went to Robins' place that night and they talked about the wedding. They were inviting family and friends, work colleagues and their friends at Alcoholics Anonymous. "What about the honeymoon?" she asked Robin. Robin replied, "I've got that all organised. We're going to Australia for three weeks. I've even got a camper van organised." Andrea gave him a huge cuddle.

Once Andrea left, Horatio said, "That means I'm going to fly, Sir." Robin replied, "It does indeed Horatio." Horatio added, "Will we be be going to Tasmania, Sir? The place that I never got to see?" Robin told him, "That's part of the plan Horatio. Sydney, Melbourne, Tasmania and back." Horatio exclaimed, "Great, Sir!"

Robin sat a map out on the kitchen bench for Horatio to see. "It certainly is a big place, Sir." Robin nodded.

At the next Alcoholics Anonymous meeting, after everybody had spoken and were having their coffee, Robin stood in the centre of the room and said, "Excuse me. I have an important announcement to make. I have asked Andrea to marry me and she has agreed." Everybody clapped and crowded in on the pair. Robin said, "There's one more thing. You and your other halves are all invited." There was a huge cheer.

Robin pulled Leroy to one side. Leroy shook his hand and congratulated him again. Robin said, "Leroy, we haven't known each other for years but you've help to save my life. I'd like you to be my best man." Leroy was shocked and speechless for a moment before saying, "You can't have me as your best man, surely there's somebody else." Robin said, "There are other people but I don't owe them my life." A huge grin crept across Leroys' face as he gave Robin another near rib-breaking bear hug. "Guess what, everybody?" shouted Leroy. "I'm the best man!" There was a huge round of applause. Andreas bridesmaid was her receptionist from work.

The wedding was four weeks away. Robin and Andrea, being lawyers, had everything organised.

The day before the wedding arrived in a flash. Andrea visited Robin and was a bundle of nerves. "What if I trip over? What if I say the wrong thing," she said. Robin spoke to her and calmed her down, reassuring her that everything was in order. "All you have to do is say I do," said Robin.

The wedding was held in the park where Andrea and Robin had visited every Saturday for seven months. When Robin and Leroy arrived, everybody was there. Friends, work colleagues and the members of Alcoholics Anonymous. They walked straight up and took their position. All that they had to do was stand there and wait.

Some fifteen minutes later the lady on the portable piano began playing 'Here Comes The Bride.' Andrea looked a picture. Robin had to try his hardest not to look around as Andrea and her bridesmaid made their way next to Robin. Robin and Andrea looked at each other and smiled.

When the Minister said his piece, Leroy reached into his pocket and Handed Robin the ring. After placing the ring on Andreas' finger, her bridesmaid handed her a ring which Andrea who slid the ring onto Robins finger. The Minister then said, "I now pronounce you man and wife. Robin, you may kiss the bride. Robin and Andrea kissed much to the delight of the clapping and cheering crowd.

As Robin and Andrea turned and walked down the aisle, the cheering and clapping got louder. There was confetti everywhere. As Andrea got in and sat down in the limousine she exclaimed, "Our suitcases!" Robin reassured her that they were in the boot.

They arrived at New York Airport with thirty minutes to spare. The pair went to respective toilets and got changed into what they thought was 'Australian' clothes. They boarded the plane and Horatio was beside himself with excitement at the prospect of flying. When the plane was in the air, Horatio spent the entire flight floating up and down the aisle looking out of the windows on both see

By this stage Horatio permanently made himsel
visible to Andrea who, along with Robin kept looking
at the excited Horatio and smiling to themselves and
each other. He did it for the entire twenty two hour
trip to Sydney, Australia while Robin and Andrea
nodded of intermittently.

When they arrived in Sydney they picked up their
suitcases when they spotted a giant of a man in a suit
wearing a hat was holding up a placard with 'Tower'
written on it. They made their way towards him. He
put the placard down and said, "G'day. I'm Neil. I'l
be taking you to your hotel. Let me take those." He
reached out and grabbed a heavy suitcase under each
arm and led them to a limousine.

On the way to the hotel, Horatios' eyes were agog at
the different dress sense and at the colour of Sydney.

On arriving at the hotel, Neil opened the limousine
door for the pair then grabbed their suitcases.
"Follow me, guys," he said. Neil went to reception
and said, "Mr. and Mrs. Tower." The receptionist
handed Robin two sets of room keys. Neil took them
to the elevator which took them to the fifteenth
storey. He sat their suitcases on the bed and wished
them an enjoyable stay.

Robin and Andrea collapsed on the bed. They were-
jet lagged. The pair slept for eight hours while
Horatio marvelled at how high they were and how the
street below appeared from that height.

Robin and Andrea slept until 10am the next day. When they came to their senses, showered and got dressed, they decided to take in the sights of Sydney. It took them five days. They went to the Opera House, caught a taxi over the Sydney Harbour Bridge, went to museums, art galleries and so forth.

When they decided it was time to leave, Robin rang a car hire company and organised a camper van. There was a knock on their door an hour later. There stood a smartly dressed young man who said, "Mr. Tower?" Robin said, "Yes." The young man handed Robin a set of keys. "Your camper van is parked out the front of the hotel, Sir."

Robin and Andrea grabbed their suitcases and put them in the back of the camper van. They were headed for Melbourne. Robin didn't fancy doing the ten hour drive in one hit so they decided to stay in the camper van at the half way mark. First they had to get out of Sydney. It took them two hours.

They arrived on the outskirts of Melbourne two days later and had the same trouble that they had in Sydney. It took them 90 minutes to get to the CBD. They stopped at the first hotel that they saw. They didn't go much on Melbourne and only spent three days there.

Robin rang and organised travel on the Spirit of Tasmania, the boat that travels from Melbourne to Devonport in Tasmania. The following afternoon they boarded the boat. They had a poor nights sleep due to the rumble of the boats engines.

When they departed, they decided to tour Tasmania anti-clockwise. They travelled down the rugged West coast, which wasn't much to look at with the exception of Cradle Mountain.

They then travelled across to the East coast via Hobart. They spent a day in Hobart but weren't overly impressed. They were, however, impressed by the East coast which was more scenic and a few degrees warmer.

They then travelled across back to Devonport. They had a day to kill. Horatio said, "Would we have time to go to Stanley? That's where we were headed before being ambushed." Robin looked at the map and said they could squeeze it in but would have to leave straight away.

When they arrived in Stanley they headed straight for the Stanley Nut, an imposing volcanic plug, towering hundreds of feet in the air. Robin and Andrea caught the chairlift up to the top while Horatio simply floated. Once at the top, the views were spectacular. Unfortunately they didn't have time to walk around it. They had to get back in time for the boat.

They arrived back in Melbourne after another noisy, sleepless night. Again, when driving from Melbourne to Sydney they stopped and camped at the half way mark.

After three hours they found the same hotel that they stayed in on arrival. They weren't due to fly out for two days but had no trouble filling in the time. Both Robin and Andrea slept for the majority of the trip so arrived in New York feeling quite fresh.

Robin and Andrea arrived back at Robins place feeling quite tired. They went and lay on their backs on Robins bed, holding hands and staring at the ceiling. After a few moments, Robin said, "Well, Mrs. Tower." Andrea replied, "Well Mr. Tower. What next?" Robin paused for a while then said, "Who's going to stay where?" After two hours they decided that Andrea would move in with Robin. "I'll have a garage sale," she said."

Two weeks later Andrea had a garage sale, selling everything except things of sentimental value. A few members from Alcoholics Anonymous attended. Andrea had everything sold in two hours.

Robin and Andrea lived in the same place until they retired. They applied and were accepted for Australian citizenship. They retired to the fishing village that they visited many years ago called Stanley.

Horatio was in his element.